D1442297

apa's Free Day PARTY

Marilyn Nelson
illustrated by Wayne Anthony Still

Special book excerpts or customized printing can also be created to fit specific needs.
For details, write or call the office of the Just Us Books special sales manager.
P.O. Box 5306 East Orange, New Jersey 07019. 973.672.7701

JUST US BOOKS and the Just Us Books logo are trademarks of Just Us Books, Inc.

ISBN: 978-0-940975-72-9
JustUsBooks.com
10 9 8 7 6 5 4 3 2 1
Printed in United States of America

"How old are you, Papa?" Johnnie asked as she curled up on her parents' bed. It was a winter evening in 1924. "Papa" John Mitchell, his wife, Ray D., and the children were chatting and laughing the quiet way toward bedtime.

Papa was sitting in his easy chair with his feet near the woodburning stove.

"How old am I? Baby, I can't rightly say," Papa replied.

"How can you not know how old you are, Papa? All you have to do is count up your birthdays."

Johnnie couldn't understand that at all. Her birthday was November first, and she was eight years, two months, and fourteen days old.

"Well," Papa said, "I figure I must be near about 60, given that I was born a year or two after freedom come in 1865. But I don't know exactly what month or day I was born on. Or even what year."

"Back when I was born, hardly anybody kept track of Black people's birthday

Just a few years before I was born, Black children could be bought and sold, just like calves and colts, just like puppies. Sometimes they couldn't even live with their families. But of course you already know that."

When I was still too little to do much work, I heard grown-up people talking about how, when they were still in bondage, they used to scrape the last morsels of cornmeal mush out of wooden bowls with wooden spoons, and whisper about how great it would be to be free. I didn't know what freedom meant."

I thought freedom must have something to do with having enough to eat."

"My father had run away to serve the right side in the war between slavery and justice. He came back with a limp, enough money to buy a few acres of uncleared land, and enough love to settle down with a wife."

"I lived the first years of my life there in a little one-room house with Ma and Pa and Willie, the baby. My world was that little house and the surrounding fields, where we all worked hard all day making things grow."

"One night when I was five or six, horses galloped up to our house, and men wearing white hoods and carrying torches and rifles set fire to our home."

"I heard Pa scream. Ma screamed, 'Run, John, run! Go north, boy! Run! Run!'"

"It was dark. I was shaking with fear. But I ran. I slowed down just long enough to look up and find the North Star and that's the direction I headed. Sometimes I stopped to drink from a creek. I stopped to sleep when it was daylight, but as soon as it got dark, I looked at the sky and started running again."

"**S**ome days and nights later, I was eating a carrot in a garden when a big white hand landed on my shoulder. I was so tired and hungry and scared that I fell down in a faint. The man picked me up and carried me into his house."

"**I** woke up lying on a bed that felt like a cloud. Two big white faces asked where I came from and what my parents' names were. I didn't know where I came from. I said my parents' names were Pa and Ma, and that ghosts on horseback set the house on fire and Ma said go north."

"Mr. and Mrs. Bryant looked at each other. Their son, Cullen, who was about my age, stood at the foot of his bed staring at me with his mouth open."

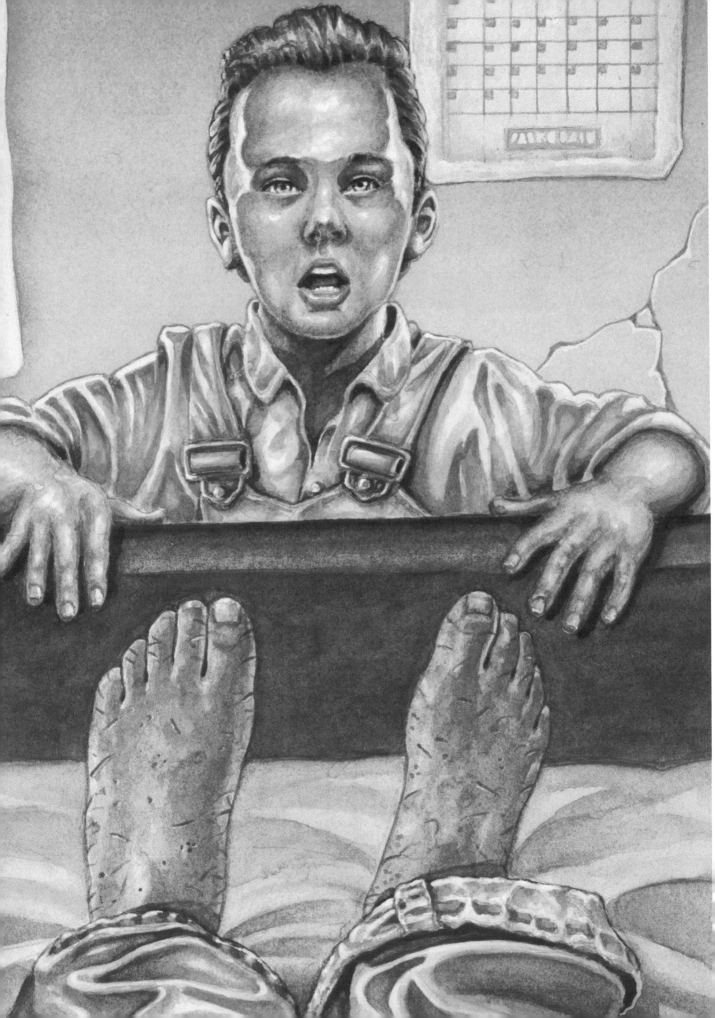

"Cullen and I grew up sharing that bedroom. We played together, sometimes we fought, and we got in trouble together, almost like brothers. Like the time we ate the peaches."

"Every summer, Mrs. Bryant canned most of the peaches from the peach trees in the yard, while Cull and I hung around with our mouths watering. One summer, when Mrs. Bryant was done canning peaches, she put the jars of canned peaches under the bed in the front room to cool while she took the buggy to a revival meeting under a tent in town."

"Mr. Bryant was keeping the Sabbath by fishing. As soon as we were alone, Cull and I went straight to the front room and opened a warm jar of canned peaches."

"In a trance of pleasure, we ate every last jar of peaches, and drank all the syrup, too. We fell asleep on the floor with round bellies and smiles."

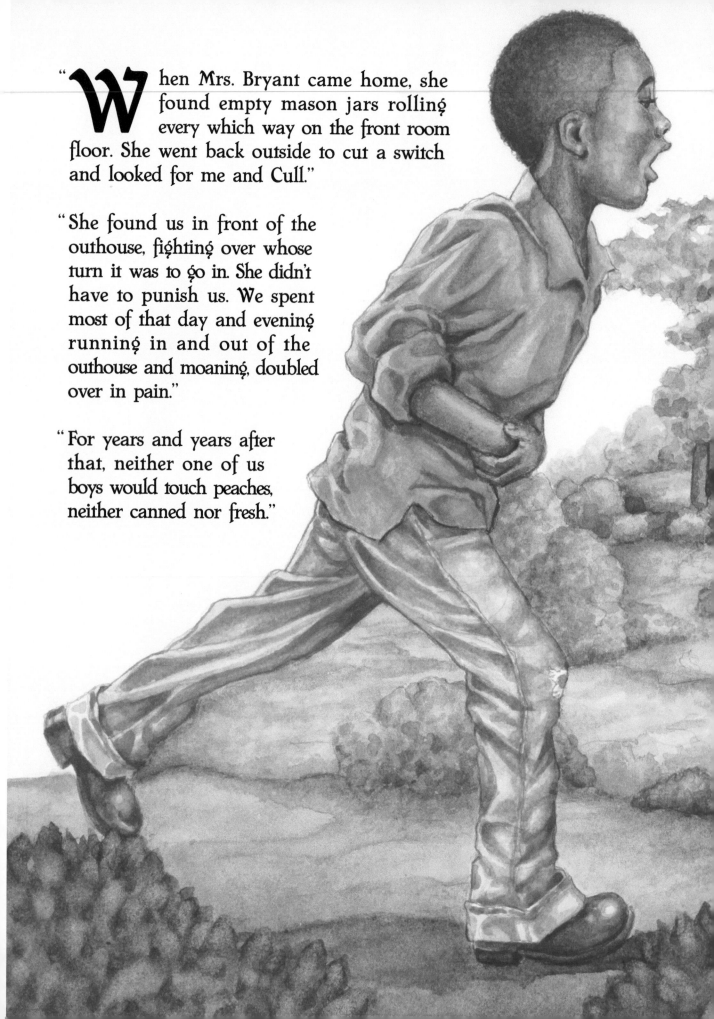

"When Mrs. Bryant came home, she found empty mason jars rolling every which way on the front room floor. She went back outside to cut a switch and looked for me and Cull."

"She found us in front of the outhouse, fighting over whose turn it was to go in. She didn't have to punish us. We spent most of that day and evening running in and out of the outhouse and moaning, doubled over in pain."

"For years and years after that, neither one of us boys would touch peaches, neither canned nor fresh."

"Cullen and I grew up to be young men and found jobs. I got a job on a ferryboat, guiding the boat back and forth across the Mississippi River between Missouri and Kentucky. One day, two strangers called me names and got up in my face and I threw them overboard. I went right home and told the Bryants what had happened."

"We all knew my life would be in danger if the men came after me. The Bryants agreed that I should leave on a train the very next day. They sent me off with some of their farm animals and enough money to buy a farm."

"I waved good-bye to the Bryants for a long time."

"My train went west toward the new state of Oklahoma. There was a town in Oklahoma called Boley that I had heard things about that I could hardly believe. I had heard that Boley was a town of people who looked like me, people who were born in bondage, or like I was, born to people who had been freed. In Boley they owned all the farms and businesses in and around town."

"When I got to Boley, I spent an hour walking up and down Pecan Street, just looking at the men and women of this miraculous free Black town. Within a few days, I bought a piece of land to farm."

"I built a house. Then, for the first time in my life, I plowed my own land, grew my own crops, and slept under my own roof at night. I milked my cow every morning."

The next evening, when they'd finished chores and settled down together, Johnnie was quiet for a long time. Then she said, "Papa, it's sad that your mama and papa weren't ever with you on your birthday. But I bet they remembered."

"Yes," Papa said. "If they survived."

He sighed, and was quiet. Then Johnnie asked, "Papa, can we GIVE you a birthday? Can we make one up? Everybody ought to have a birthday cake!"

"I already have me a made-up birthday," Papa answered. "The Bryants always celebrated my birthday on April 9, the day Lee surrendered to Grant at Appomattox and the war for freedom was won. On that day slavery was pretty much all-she-wrote. Mr. and Mrs. Bryant used to give me a little present every April 9."

"I remember one year they gave me a pretty little pearl-handled jackknife. I had that knife for years. Don't know what happened to it."

"But that's not your birthday," Johnnie said. "That's your Free Day. Can we have a Free Day Party for you, then, Papa? With a cake and frosting and sweet tea and a red balloon?"

"Yes, indeedy," John laughed. "With cake and frosting and sweet tea and a red balloon!"

But when April 9 came, Johnnie and Rufus were just getting over the chickenpox, Charlie B. had had a quarrel with her boyfriend, and Mama Ray D. had to teach all day. Nobody remembered to bake a cake.

That afternoon, Papa was outside brushing Prince and putting him in his stall. The rest of the family huddled together. They had to think of something fast!

"There's plenty of flour in the barrel," Johnnie said.

"But there won't be any eggs until morning," Charlie B. said.
"And you can't make a cake without eggs."

"Can we make a pie?" Johnnie asked.

"Nobody has a birthday PIE," Rufus laughed.

"This isn't Papa's birthday, anyway, smarty-pants!" Johnnie
said. "It's his FREE day!"

"Well, I reckon we'll have to make a pie," Charlie B. said. "But there's only a few skinny little sweet potatoes left, and there's no fruit at all. And it's too late to take the buggy into town to buy something to put in a pie."

"Well, we do have that jar of canned peaches Sister Washington gave me last July," Ray D. said.

"But Papa HATES peaches!" Rufus said, recalling the famous Day of the Belly-Aches.

"I can't think of anything else," Ray D. sighed. "Looks like it's peach pie or nothing. I'll make a crust as soon as I change my clothes and get out of these shoes."

When supper was over Charlie B. brought the pie to the table in a cloud of fragrant steam and set it in front of Papa. Little bubbles of amber juice peeked through its golden crust. It was a beautiful pie. But it was a PEACH pie. And everybody knew that John Mitchell HATED peaches. Would this Free Day pie make him happy? Would he eat it? Would it make him sick?

Ray D. and the children sang, "Happy Free Day to you!"

Papa sat there beaming. Then he cut the Free Day pie.

Ray D., Charlie B., Johnnie, and Rufus held their breath. Papa raised the first forkful of pie, blew on it, and put it into his mouth. He chewed very slowly. A faraway look grew in his eyes. They watched him eat another bite.

After he'd scraped the last morsels off his plate, he put his fork down and leaned back in his chair.

Folding his hands across his belly, Papa smiled toward the ceiling and said, "That was the best danged pie I ever ate! Nothing improves the taste of food more than freedom."

PAPA'S FREE DAY

VOLUME 1. NUMBER 1   BOLEY, OKLAHOMA   2 CENTS

AFTERWORD

This book is based on stories my mother told about her father's unusual boyhood with the Bryants of Dorena, Missouri, and his adult years (her childhood) spent on his farm near the independent and successful all-Black town of Boley, Oklahoma.

Dorena is right across the Mississippi River from Hickman, Kentucky. John's wife, my grandmother, Ray D. Atwood, was from Hickman. Every few years the Atwoods had a little reunion in the family's homeplace. Late in his life my Uncle Rufus told me that one year, as a middle-aged man visiting Hickman for a reunion, he decided to go across the river to Dorena and see if any of the Bryants, whom his father had often spoken of, were still living. On Dorena's main street he saw a sign: "Bryant's Department Store." He parked his car, went in, and asked a cashier if Mr. Bryant was in. He was directed to an office upstairs. He knocked on the door.

A white man who looked to be in his fifties opened it. Uncle Rufus said, "You don't know me, but I think maybe your people raised my father." The white man exclaimed, "Oh, my God! You're John's son? I'm Cullen's son!" He threw his arms around Uncle Rufus.

"My dad told so many stories about your dad," they both said. They went back across the river together, to the reunion.

For many years the thread of family connection was dropped and virtually forgotten. But in 2020 I wrote to the Missouri Historical Society and asked for help finding the descendants of the Bryants. And voila! I found them! They know the story! They have a letter Uncle Rufus wrote to Cull's son some 45 years ago. On September 27, 2020 our families met via Zoom. We agreed that we feel we've found long-lost relatives.

– Marilyn Nelson

(Top right) John Mitchell, my grandfather, was called Papa by his children, Rufus, Charlie B. and my mother, Johnnie.

(Bottom right) Standing man: W. C. "Cull" Bryant, Sr. Standing boy: W.C. Bryant, Jr. Baby: a cousin, name unknown.

(Above left) My mother, Johnnie Edwina Mitchell, and her brother, Rufus Cornelius Mitchell. Their mother, Ray Diverne Atwood Mitchell, was a teacher in the Boley School and in the Boley Creek-Seminole College. (Above right) The Boley Rodeo and BBQ Festival, featuring one of the nation's few all-Black rodeos, has been held every Memorial Day weekend (except 2020) since 1903.

(Center right) The Farmers and Merchants Bank was the site of a 1932 attempted bank robbery by associates of the gangster, Pretty Boy Floyd. The heist was unsuccessful because citizens of Boley defended their bank.

Pecan Street (left) was where many businesses were located. Boley was one of approximately 50 all-Black towns and settlements founded in the Oklahoma territory between 1865 and 1920. Established in 1903, Boley, during its height, had more than 4,000 citizens, a number of Black-owned businesses, a post office, a public school, a newspaper, two colleges, an electric power plant and one of the first chartered Black banks in the United States.

ABOUT THE CREATORS

Marilyn Nelson was born in Cleveland, Ohio, the daughter of a teacher and an Air Force officer who was a member of the last graduating class of Tuskegee Airmen. Her maternal grandfather, after losing his parents, was raised by the couple who found him. He and his wife made their home on a farm near the all-Black town of Boley, Oklahoma. She is the author or translator of more than 20 books and chapbooks for adults and children.

Her critically acclaimed books for young adults include, among others, *A Wreath for Emmett Till, Fortune's Bones, My Seneca Village*, and the ground-breaking *Carver: A Life in Poem* a Newbery Honor Book and recipient of the Boston Globe/Hornbook and the Flora Stieglit Straus Awards. Her memoir, *How I Discovered Poetry*, written in a series of 50 poems, is a Coretta Scott King Honor Book and was named one of NPR's Best Books of 2014. She is a three-time finalist for the National Book Award, and her many honors include the Frost Medal, the Ruth Lilly Poetry Prize, the NSK Neustadt Award, and fellowships from the Guggenheim Foundation and the National Endowment for the Arts.

A professor emerita of English at the University of Connecticut, a former Chancellor of the Academy of American Poets, and a former Poet-in-Residence of the American Poets Corne at the Cathedral of St. John the Divine, Marilyn Nelson was Poet Laureate of Connecticut, 2001 - 2006.

Website: www.marilyn-nelson.com

Wayne Anthony Still is an award-winning illustrator, designer, painter and sculptor. He holds a bachelor of fine arts degree in illustration and graphic design from the University of the Arts in Philadelphia, Pennsylvania, and has completed graduate work toward a master's degree in painting at Temple University in Pennsylvania.

Mr. Still says, "My creativity is driven by my passion for detail, and I thrive on challenges tha allow me to excel. I enjoy creating art that will touch the heart, mind and soul of the masse giving them cause to think and reflect; and through this experience, I hope my expression as an artist brings joy as well as enlightenment."

Mr. Still's work includes exquisitely designed figurines, collector's stamps for internationa governments, masterful plates as well as illustrations and paintings.

He makes his home in Pennsylvania near the city of Philadelphia where another famous member of his family, William Still, was an active leader and conductor-historian of the Underground Railroad.

Website: www.wayneanthonystill.com

Photo credits:
p. 30 top right, courtesy Marilyn Nelson; bottom right, W.C. Bryant
p. 31 top left, courtesy Marilyn Nelson; top right, center right and bottom, Oklahoma Historical Society